Passive Income Stream Generator

Top 10 Ways to Financial Freedom

Copyright 2017 by C.J. ELLIOTT - All rights reserved.

The follow eBook is reproduced below with the goal of providing information that is as accurate and reliable as possible. Regardless, purchasing this eBook can be seen as consent to the fact that both the publisher and the author of this book are in no way experts on the topics discussed within and that any recommendations or suggestions that are made herein are for entertainment purposes only. Professionals should be consulted as needed prior to undertaking any of the action endorsed herein.

This declaration is deemed fair and valid by both the American Bar Association and the Committee of Publishers Association and is legally binding throughout the United States.

Furthermore, the transmission, duplication or reproduction of any of the following work including specific information will be considered an illegal act irrespective of if it is done electronically or in print. This extends to creating a secondary or tertiary copy of the work or a recorded copy and is only allowed with express written consent from the Publisher. All additional right reserved.

The information in the following pages is broadly considered to be a truthful and accurate account of facts and as such any inattention, use or misuse of the information in question by the reader will render any resulting actions solely under their purview. There are no scenarios in which the publisher or the original author of this work can be in any fashion deemed liable for any hardship or damages that may befall them after undertaking information described herein.

Additionally, the information in the following pages is intended only for informational purposes and should thus be thought of as universal. As befitting its nature, it is presented without assurance regarding its prolonged validity or interim quality. Trademarks that are mentioned are done without written consent and can in no way be considered an endorsement from the trademark holder.

Introduction

Congratulations on downloading Passive Income Stream Generator: Top 10 Ways to Financial Freedom and thank you for doing so. It doesn't matter if you are looking for an escape from your 9-to-5 or looking for a way to save for retirement, passive income is the answer. It definitely takes more than wanting it to make it happen, however, which is why so many people give up before they have seen a single red cent.

Luckily, the following chapters will discuss everything you need to know to start generating real results from a wide variety of passive income streams, and also explain how you can stick with them in order to see the best results in the shortest period of time possible. First, you will learn how to generate passive income from traditional methods like investing in rental properties or the stock market. Then you will learn about a variety of different online options including running an online business, affiliate marketing, retail arbitrage, creating digital content, authoring eBooks, selling stock photos and advertising on an Instagram account.

While all of these options are guaranteed to generate passive income in the long term, it is important to keep in mind that it won't happen overnight. Generating a passive income stream takes hard work and dedication up front, so that you can enjoy the fruits of your labours early on. If you are looking for a get rich quick scheme, you are better off saving yourself some time and looking elsewhere instead. If you stick with them, however, you have the potential to make up to thousands of dollars a month with little or no additional effort, you just need to stick with it.

There are plenty of books on this subject on the market, thanks again for choosing this one! Every effort was made to ensure it is full of as much useful information as possible, please enjoy!

Chapter 1: Real Estate

When it comes to passive income, there are few more reliable means than investing in real estate for the purposes of renting it out; after all as Mark Twain once observed, they aren't making any more land. However, while there will always be some property out there that you can make a profit on, it is going to take a significant financial investment up front in order to generate the best return on your investment. If you can manage to pull it off, however, it will reliably generate a return on investment that surpasses practically any other investment strategy while building your portfolio at the same time.

As actively managing both tenants and the upkeep on your rental properties isn't exactly passive, if you decide to go down this route then you are going to want to look into finding a property management company to take care of your rental property for you. This, in turn, limits you primarily to condos or apartment complexes as a majority of property management companies aren't going to be interested in managing single, single-family properties. While this will naturally mean a decrease in your profits, it will mean significantly less work as well.

Condominium: Purchasing a condominium is a great choice for new real estate owners as it automatically comes with a property management team in place. Additionally, they are typically going to be a good deal cheaper than other types of property. Furthermore, you will typically attract younger, upwardly mobile tenants who will treat the property well and have little trouble paying the rent on time. On the other hand, you are likely to make less overall with them, both because the rent is typically going to be less than other property types and also because you are going to make less from appreciation as the value of condos rise more slowly than single family homes.

Small apartment complexes: Small apartment complexes are another good type of starter rental property as their size means you won't have to take on too much all at once. Additionally, if the property doesn't already have a contract with an existing property management company you can often find someone to live on site and provide these services in exchange for free housing. Additionally, they are often considered quite reliable as you will have several different people paying rent all at once which means it is unlikely they will all be unable or unwilling to pay at all at the same time.

The biggest downside to these types of properties is that the type of individuals who currently live there typically limits your future tenant prospects. If the previous landlord did their due diligence and found quality tenants then you are golden, if they rented to questionable individuals then you will have trouble attracting respectable tenants until the others move out.

Finding the right property: When it comes to choosing the right property for you, the first thing you are going to need to do is to consider various neighbourhoods that look promising for rental properties based on local conditions. This means looking for neighbourhoods that have access to amenities that renters would be interested that are also close to areas that offer a wide range of jobs. As you are going to most likely be looking to attract single individuals instead of families, amenities like local nightlife and easy access to public transportation.

Once you have determined what you are looking for, you are going to want to do some legwork and visit potential neighbourhoods both during the day and at night in order to ensure the neighbourhood doesn't change dramatically between the two. You should also make a point of talking to current renters in the area to see what they think of it as a whole. Renters will always give you a more honest response, as they have no real stake in the area.

You will also want to do your research and determine what the property tax in the area is like when compared to the area as a whole. It is important to research exactly where you are looking as property taxes can vary dramatically, even in neighbourhoods that are right next to one another.

Confirming the right rental price: Once you find a property that you are interested in, the next thing you are going to want to do is run the numbers and ensure that it is legitimately going to be worth your time and effort to move forward based on the potential return. This means you are going to want to look at what other rents in the area are like before factoring in anything that makes your property unique, and thus worth more or less than the average. With that number in mind you will then need to factor in the cost you will pay for insurance, your loan payment, taxes and property management fees and then subtract all of that from the amount you will pay for rent.

The amount that is left over from this exercise is going to be what you can expect to make each month on rent. You are going to also want to assume that the property is going to sit empty for at least one month each year to account for periods where a renter has moved out and another has yet to move in. From there, you will then need to subtract out another 10 percent to account for things like missed payments and repairs that you will have to make each year. If the amount left over seems like it would be worth your time then you know you have a property that is worth moving forward with.

Move forward with a plan: Before you start looking at properties you are going to need to have a clear idea what type of loan you will qualify for, what your cash on hand is looking like and if you are going to be looking into hard money or dealer financing loans. Moving forward with a clear plan in mind will make it easier to limit your search to reasonable properties and make it easier for you to negotiate successfully once you have found something that works for you.

Chapter 2: Financial Investing

Choosing to invest in stocks that pay out dividends is a great way to generate a passive income stream. Although it is somewhat riskier than trading stocks as you have to hold the stocks you choose for a greater period of time in order to turn a profit. A dividend is paid out by the company in question to its shareholders on a set schedule and is based on the amount of profit the company has seen over a given period of time. Dividends can come in the form of stock, cash or even property, though this last is less common. Stable companies whose stock does not tend to move much offer dividends as a way to retain, entice and reward shareholders.

As an added benefit, as most dividend paying stocks come from companies that are financially stable, their stock price tends to rise in the long run which means an increase in the dividend payments over time. A company that pays consistently improving dividends is typically going to be a firm that is financially healthy and generates a consistent cash flow. These types of companies are typically extremely stable which means their stock prices are going to be less volatile than the market as a whole. This means that they are typically going to be lower risk than companies that have more volatile price movements, though the potential for holding onto their stock is going to be lower as well.

Another benefit of dividends is the potential to reinvest them back into the dividend producing company, leading to even greater returns in the long run. Many dividend producing companies allow their shareholders to take their payouts in the form of additional shares of stock in the company which is a great choice if you are looking to generate passive income in the long term as it means future payments are going to be even larger when you are ready to capitalize on them.

Dividend investing rules

Finding success with dividend investing isn't rocket science, but it does require an understanding of a handful of basic rules, which are outlined below.

Quality supersedes quantity: Perhaps the most important consideration when it comes to choosing stocks with the goal of dividend investment in mind is the rate of dividend yield. Simply put, the greater the yield, the higher the return. However, the numbers can be surprisingly deceptive if you don't know what you are looking for. Specifically, this means you are going to want to make sure that a given company's current payout level is in line with what they have paid out in the past as unsustainable payout levels means there is a chance that the company could stop paying dividends in the future as they are typically given out at the discretion of the company, with no guarantee that they will continue forever.

This means that it is important to look for companies that have a history of paying out regular dividends over the long term as opposed to those that simply offer the highest return at the moment. If you are looking for a buy-and-hold investment then the income generated by low risk dividend stocks will always trump higher amounts in the short term, given a long enough time period.

Avoid new companies: When looking for reliable dividends, you are going to want to stick with those that have earned dividend aristocrat status. Dividend aristocrat status is given out to companies that have given out increasing dividends to stockholders every year, for at least 25 years. These are typically easily recognized brands that always generate a reliable cash flow and have very high odds of continuing to do so in the future.

Be aware of growth potential: In addition to keeping an eye on past returns in comparison to current offerings, it is also important to look to the future potential of a given company before choosing the right dividend-producing stock for you. This is also the main difference between value investing and growth investing. With growth investing, there is less importance placed on where a stock is currently sitting and more emphasis on where it is going to be in the long term. This long-term view will typically give you a much better picture of what its dividend payouts are going to be.

Consider the payout ratio: The dividend payout ratio of a company will often tell you how safe the investment is going to be overall. This ratio measure how much income the company in question is going to retain compared to how much they are currently paying out to their shareholders. Being aware of this number will allow you to tread cautiously around stocks with a high-yield dividend that initially looks promising, but in reality, is taking up a large portion of the given company's profits to generate. In these scenarios, it would only take a small reduction in the company's income stream in order to see the dividend return rate decrease substantially.

Diversify: While concentrating your investment focus on a handful of profitable stocks or a profitable market sector makes sense when the market is strong, it also leaves you vulnerable to market downturns. As this is a long-term strategy then it stands to reason the sector of the market you have chosen to focus on will see this type of downturn a few times before you are ultimately ready to sell off your holdings. This means it is important to diversify the types of stocks you are holding onto in order to ensure that these inevitable downturns impact your passive income stream as little as possible. If dividend payments are then reduced in one area you will have the added security of knowing they are less likely to be reduced across the board which means a majority of your investments will always be safe.

Know when to bow out: While dividend investing is all about taking the long-term view of the stocks you invest in, it is important to keep in mind the difference between taking a long-term view and holding on to a sinking ship. While it is perfectly fine to hold onto the stock of a company that has a history of long-term success who then has a bad year, it is never a good idea to continue holding onto stock in a company that misses its growth goals for more than one year in a row. Missing target growth goals is a sure sign that dividends are going to decrease and the longer you hold onto the related stock, the less you will get for it when you do decide it is time to sell.

Chapter 3: Online Business

If you are looking for a way to start your own online business in a way that will generate relatively passive income, then Fulfilment by Amazon (FBA) is a good place to start. As an FBA member, you find products that you are interested in selling through whatever means you decide upon and then send these items to the nearest Amazon distribution centre where they stay until they are sold at which point Amazon ships them off to the buyer without you having to lift a finger. Amazon then also takes on the workload related to dealing with customer service issues as well. In return, they charge you for storage, shipping and take a cut of the profit from the sale. There is also a monthly $40 fee required to utilize the service.

In addition to letting Amazon do a majority of the work, being an FBA member has two other major benefits. First, the items that you sell are automatically eligible for Amazon Prime shipping, which means that the millions of Amazon Prime members out there are going to choose your item over a competitor's item even if the competition has a slightly better price. Second, your items will naturally show up higher in the search results which means customers might not even see the competition to begin with.

Maximizing potential

As there is a monthly fee to be an FBA user, it is important to do everything you can to ensure your store makes enough to justify the cost. The following are a list of ways you can do just that.

Choose the right items to sell: First and foremost, even though Amazon is doing most of the work, you are still going to be the face of your store which means you are going to want to do everything in your power to ensure your store rating is as high as possible. This means you are only going to want to stock high quality, reliable items, otherwise customers won't be able to trust that their purchase will be worth their time.

In order to maximize your profits, the first thing you are going to want to do is to download the Amazon Seller Application. This application offers extremely useful functionality in that it allows you to enter the specifics for any product you are hoping to sell and show you how much you will make off of it once all the relevant fees are subtracted from it. It also allows you to determine how many other people are currently selling the same or similar items on Amazon and what they are charging as well. Finally, it shows which versions of a given product, or which brand, is currently the most popular with Amazon customers so you can make your purchasing choices accordingly.

Additionally, before you go ahead and pull the trigger on a given product you are going to want to visit the site CamelCamelCamel.com or one like it. This site provides details relating to how a given product's popularity is trending on Amazon. It shows a detailed graph of the prices that people have been willing to pay for a product over a set period of time which will allow you to determine if a product is growing in popularity (price increasing) or becoming less popular (price decreasing).

Find a niche: While many individuals do fine with stores that sell a wide variety of different products, choosing a niche of products to focus on will allow you to do more accurate research when it comes to determining what types of products to sell. Settling on a niche means you will be able to more easily pinpoint the likes and dislikes of your target audience while also narrowing down ways to find products in that niche for the best prices popular. The best niches are those that have a decent sized following, but are not yet so popular that you are going to be competing with thousands of other FBA members for each and every potential sale.

Take advantage of good deals: While finding a niche will make it easier to find the best products at the best prices in the long run, the number one rule of being success with FBA is that if you find a product that you can make a large profit on, then you should sell it, regardless of what that product happens to be. As such, if you find a product that is currently selling in the real world for one-fourth of the price that it is currently selling for on Amazon then you should buy it as this practically guarantees you are going to net a solid profit once all the fees are taken into account. This is the best way to ensure that this type of passive income stream remains truly passive. When you find these types of deals it is important to have the capital on hand to capitalize on them fully, as it is unlikely they are going to stick around for the long term.

Utilize reward systems: While simply purchasing products cheaply and then selling them for a profit is a perfectly valid strategy, if you want to maximize your benefits from FBA, there is still more you can be doing. First, if you qualify, you are going to want to ensure that you make as many of your purchases as possible with a credit card that generates rewards for purchases. You can then use this card to by gift cards for specific stores and products through sites like GiftCardZen.com. You can then generate money back offers by purchasing items through Ebates.com.

Additionally, you are going to want to keep an eye on websites like RetailMeNot.com and FatWallet.com that offer a variety of coupon codes for things like additional discounts and coupon codes. When purchasing products in the real world you will want to be aware of offers from retail chains such as Kohl's which offer a separate rewards program of their own for repeat customers.

As an example, you could easily purchase a $100 gift card for $90 and then make purchases through Ebates.com to save an additional $3, which is already almost $15 worth of extra profit. You can then save as much as $30 through the judicious use of coupon codes and earn $10 from various rewards programs which drops a $100 purchase down to just $45.

Chapter 4: Affiliate Marketing

If you are already part of an online community that is based around a hobby or interest then you can likely leverage that community into an affiliate marketing-based passive income stream. Affiliate marketing is a type of dedicated advertising where you work with companies or other types of merchants for the purpose of helping them sell their products in return for a cut of the profits of every item sold. This passive income stream requires a bit of work to set up effectively, but it can generate a constant stream of profit when done correctly.

Find a niche: The first thing you are going to need to do is to consider the type of customers you are going to be marketing to. As previously mentioned, if you have a hobby that people are dedicated too then this is a good place to start as you are going to be spending a good deal of time with products related to the niche and having an interest in them beside money making will make the process easier in the long run. If you don't have an idea already in mind then you should choose a hobby for people with a good amount of discretionary income and a steady stream of new products always coming to the market.

Do some research: With a niche in mind, the next thing you are going to want to do is to take some time and visit existing websites where these types of individuals spend their time. You are going to want to consider the types of things that are important to them and the type of products they are likely to buy the most frequently. It is important to take note of their thought processes, the things that are important to them and the slang they use. Sounding like you are one of them is key to making them trust your opinion when you tell them to buy one product over another.

Create a website: In order for this passive income stream to work, you are going to need a blog where you can collect your thoughts and your affiliate marketing articles. When creating your site, keep in mind the types of things you saw on the sites you researched and strive to create a space that members of your niche are going to feel comfortable in. Additionally, you are going to want to create content that is more than just advertisements to ensure that niche members are going to want to get in the habit of visiting your site on the regular.

Affiliate programs: While there are plenty of different companies that offer affiliate programs, the easiest to get started with is Amazon. Once you sign up to be an Amazon affiliate you can choose to sell practically any product you want and they will send you a unique link to that product. Then, whenever a purchase is made through that link, you will receive a commission for the sale. Many new affiliate marketers go straight for the big-ticket items, as the commission on these will naturally be higher than with cheaper products.

This is a mistake, however, as it takes much more convincing to get someone to spend several hundred dollars on an item compared to something that is in the fifty-dollar range. When looking for items to sell, quantity is almost always going to trump quality. Another good route to take is to find items that are already discounted on Amazon and let your readers know that if they click on the link you provided they would get a discount on the item in question. Remember, your goal is to close the deal as quickly as possible because even if your review sways a customer in a given direction, if they have to think about the purchase before making it then it is less likely they are going to use your link to do so, which means you won't get credit for your hard work.

Making the sale: When it comes to convincing visitors to your site to purchase things, it is important to do your due diligence with the item in question which means purchasing it for yourself first. As an affiliate marketer, your word is your business, which means that if you promote low quality items then your total conversions are likely to drop and will be unlikely to rise again. If you purchase a product and it isn't worth the money, be sure to write about that as well, having negative product reviews as well as positive ones will make the positive reviews you do write more believable.

When using the product, be sure to take plenty of pictures of yourself doing so. Seeing the product in use will make it easier for readers to picture themselves using the product. Each review should include a breakdown of the product describing its pros and cons, but still leaving out a bit of relevant information to ensure that the reader is more likely to click the link you provide (several times throughout the review) to find the information that you left out. Once they are on the purchase page they will be more likely to go ahead and pull the trigger.

Another good option is to talk about the product's strengths but then discuss how it is too complicated for all but the most knowledgeable users, as this will make some users even more likely to purchase it. You will also want to try and create a story around each product, discuss what you were doing while using it and generally give readers as many different ways to connect with the product as possible.

Additionally, it is important to ensure that you market yourself as well as the products you are trying to sell as the more your regular readers feel that you (or a persona you create for this purpose) are an expert in a given field, the greater the weight your reviews will have when they are making up their minds whether or not to purchase a product. The more you go out of the way to make readers relate to you on a personal level, the more they will listen to you when you say that a given product is superior to its competition.

Chapter 5: REITs

If you are interested in the idea of investing in real estate but don't like the idea of dealing with the trouble of finding rental property to purchase, then investing in Real Estate Investment Trusts (REITs) might be more your speed. With this passive income stream, you don't need to worry about having lots of cash already on hand for a large down payment and can get started with virtually any amount. This is because when you invest in REITs you are investing in individual shares the same way you would as if you were investing in a company via buying into their stock. This means, instead of worrying if a given property is ultimately going to turn a profit, all you need to do is choose an REIT that has a proven track record and let their team of analysts make profitable decisions for you. In return for your investment, you will receive dividends just as you would if you invested in dividend producing stocks.

Investing in REITs does have its own drawbacks, however, as it typically requires you to pay taxes on the dividends you receive in addition to paying taxes on the income used to purchase your shares in the first place. If you are hoping to generate passive income as a retirement strategy, however, then you can negate this double taxation by putting the money into an IRA account and agreeing not to touch the funds until you are ready to retire.

REITs were created in the 1960s as a way for the average working individual to partake in the profits generated by larger real estate investments such as hotels and major office complexes, to that end they are required to ensure that 90 percent of their profits return to the shareholders and that more than five individuals control 50 percent of the available shares. Each shareholder then receives an amount of the profits based on the number of shares they hold with no preferential treatment given to those who own more shares. What's more, if you don't like the direction the REIT you have invested in is moving then you are free to sell your shares on the open market at any time with no penalty for doing so. Share prices fluctuate, just like stocks, and you will always have access to the current share price in the moment so you can make the most informed decision possible at any given time.

Types of REITs

There are many different types of REITs to choose from, based around different types of property acquisition. A brief explanation of the pros and cons of each is outlined below.

Residential REITs: The most common type of REIT that you will find focuses on residential properties. They typically invest in apartment complexes with hundreds of units or entire condominium communities rather than individual units. This is the easiest type of REIT to start with, as the basics are easy for even the uninformed to understand. They can make decisions on whether a specific REIT is successful by simply visiting the area where the holdings are located and determining what the competition is like in the area along with how full the current holdings currently are. The general rule is that the emptier space in the holding in question the weaker the REITs position currently is. It is also important to be aware of any new construction that is taking place in the area, as additional housing options will hurt the REIT's investments as well.

Retail REITs: These REITs typically specialize in either shopping centers or shopping malls, though the latter is becoming increasingly rare. This is another situation where a little bit of feet-on-the-ground investigation can easily tell you how the holdings are doing, and thus how likely the REIT is to see share prices move in the desired direction. Another good thing about these types of investment is that it is unlikely that they will have to deal with an unexpected influx of new competition as new construction in this sector is relatively sparse and requires a great deal of preplanning which means a look at local town hall meetings should be enough to tell you what to expect.

Industrial and office REITS: These two types of REITs are often grouped together simply because the leasing terms of tenants are typically much longer than with other types of REITs. Additionally, they are both more likely to experience success or failure in the present based on conditions that occurred in the past. If they experienced an influx of new tenants when space was at a premium then they are likely to exceed projections while the current leases are in place. Meanwhile, if there was plenty of space to go around at this time then they are likely to be operating with profit projections that are somewhat more modest.

Hotel and Resort REITs: These types of REITs typically show the greatest amount of profit per share, when they are profitable, though the buy-in is typically going to be the highest of any of the other REIT types as well. They are very rarely going to be subject to unexpected competition because the requirements for building something on this scale are going to require plenty of permits which will give the REIT plenty of notice that things might be changing in the future. The biggest downside to these REITs is that they are the least recession proof of any REIT as this type of expense is the first that many people cut out of their budget when things get tight.

Storage REITs: On the other end of the spectrum you have REITs that focus exclusively on business that sell storage space. They typically have the lowest overall buy-in costs. Additionally, while their dividends are typically going to be lower than most other REITs, they have proven to be extremely reliable regardless of the current state of the economy.

Chapter 6: Retail Arbitrage

If you are interested in selling physical items online and don't want to go to the hassle of opening your own online store then retail arbitrage might be for you. Originally an exclusive to those who traded in the foreign exchange currency market, arbitrage is simply the idea of purchasing a commodity at one price and then selling it elsewhere for a higher price. The rise of online marketplaces means that anyone can participate in retail arbitrage, as long as they are able to purchase items at a price that means they can be resold elsewhere for a profit.

Starting out: The biggest asset when it comes to retail arbitrage is a good nose for a great bargain. Your two biggest assets in this quest are going to be the Amazon Price check app and the eBay seller's application as these two sites are typically going to be the best place to go to sell your items for a profit. Both of these applications will help you determine the baseline price an item is selling for so you can decide if the price you are considering purchasing it at is worth the trouble.

In addition to these free applications, you are also going to want to consider the Profit Bandit application. While it has a $10 up front cost, it provides you with a wide variety of information that the free apps lack. Specifically, it will tell you how the current price of an item stacks up to the price of that item overall and also if the product is being sold by Amazon directly or if it violates their code of conduct and why. It will also tell you how much profit you stand to make off of an item based on the amount you are paying, the amount you will sell it for and any extraneous costs that might be incurred.

Finding the best items: When it comes to finding the right items to sell, many people automatically think of big-ticket items, under the rationale that, if they can be found on sale, then the profit would be substantial. While these types of items will occasionally pan out, you will almost always find a more reliable return on basic items that everyone needs as they will sell faster and more readily is found for a discounted price. While this isn't the most exciting advice, products like batteries, diapers and ink cartridges are always going to be able to ensure that your retail arbitrage business turns a profit.

While they won't necessarily sell right away, a great type of product to consider selling is seasonal items such as Halloween or Christmas decorations. These items can typically be picked up for pennies on the dollar in the days immediately following the holiday and if you are willing to wait almost a year to sell them, will always return a reliable profit, especially if you wait to a week or so before the holiday to post them for sale. The downside with this being you only have a limited window in order to ensure that the item sells or else you have to hold onto it for another entire year.

Another good choice is to keep your ear to the ground when it comes to new trends and then purchase a large amount of the new hot item in bulk before the price catches up to its new level of popularity. For example, these days' kids are all about fidget spinners that have lead the price of many versions of this product to increase dramatically. If you had hopped onto the fidget spinner bandwagon early on, then you could now sell them for a significant profit.

Finally, items from the dollar store that feature popular licensed characters such as Disney princesses or Marvel superheroes are always going to be able to turn a profit. While these products might not sell for much more than their purchase price at the moment, if you wait until a specific product is hard to find, typically four to six months, then you can easily sell it for five times what you paid for it to parents who are desperate for new content for their child who has already consumed everything else with their favorite character's face on the box.

Additional concerns: Outside of just looking for the best deals, you are also going to want to special attention to how a given item is likely to ship before buying in bulk. Keeping this factor in mind will make it easier to prevent a rash of returns on products that are exceedingly fragile or are otherwise difficult or exceedingly costly to ship. Furthermore, you will want to avoid items that are going to be complicated to ship as, if things go well, you will be shipping them out on an exceedingly frequent basis.

With these types of items, a good rule of thumb is to only move forward with sales that will net you at least 50 percent profit on the sold item. The only exception to this rule is if you have a specific idea in mind for the product when you purchase it and don't mind making less from it overall.

eBay to Amazon arbitrage: If you are looking to get into arbitrage without having to purchase any physical products, then you can actually play eBay and Amazon against one another. Specifically, what you do is spend time searching both eBay and Amazon for specific items and then, once you find a product that is selling for more on eBay, simply post a new auction and then, once it ends, purchase the product on Amazon and send it to the winner of the auction as a gift. While Amazon currently frowns upon this, it is not, strictly speaking, breaking any laws.

When it comes to completing this type of arbitrage sale successfully, it is important to ensure that the items you choose aren't on sale on Amazon for an exceedingly limited time as once an auction has been won it is difficult to get out of sending an item, even if you aren't going to make any money for it. Additionally, it is important to always only post a single auction at a time. Not only will this prevent you from losing money if the price changes on Amazon, it will make the buyer more likely to pull the trigger because of the apparent level of scarcity that having only one option provides.

Chapter 7: Webinars

While creating digital content that other people are legitimately interested in purchasing can take more time and cost more money upfront than selling physical products, eventually you will reach a point where the profit is rolling in without having to do nearly as much work. When you factor in the fact that you don't have to deal with shipping or storage costs, it may even be the more profitable option. While creating the content itself doesn't necessarily need to be terribly time consuming, you will need to spend a good deal of time marketing yourself if you hope to be successful in the long run.

Finding the right topic: In order to create a successful webinar, the first thing you will want to do is to determine what hobbies, talents and skills you are intimately familiar enough with to ensure that other people would be willing to hear you talk about them. It is important to be fluent enough in a given topic that you can provide insight greater than what can currently be found on YouTube regarding the topic for free. This means you not only need to know the topic inside and out, you need to be able to clearly and concisely teach it to others as well.

If nothing immediately comes to mind, the first thing you will want to do is to make a list of all your best skills. Almost everyone has something that they are adept at enough in order to generate at least one webinar, these skills can just be hard to see because you do them well without thinking about it. These topics can be anything from general self-help and how-to topics to more specific things that many people often think of as innate skills such as time management or organizational skills. If you are so good at something that you don't think of it right away then this is likely a good candidate for a webinar.

Express your content clearly: With a viable topic in mind, the next thing you are going to need to do is determine the best way to express your topic in a way that makes it easy for other people to follow along. Depending on the topic you choose, this could be something as simple as recording yourself talking about the topic while doing it or it could be more complicated and including some type of PowerPoint presentation. While the exact way you go about explaining your content doesn't matter, it is important that the visual and audio quality is professional, after all you want to come off as an expert in the field, not someone who is trying to make extra money off of a YouTube video recorded on their phone.

Build a website: Once you create your content, it is important that you find a place to put it online that adds to the entire experience. This means you are going to want to do more than simply throw up a link to the video and a link to PayPal, you are also going to need to create free content that makes visitors interested in seeing what's behind the pay wall. This means creating plenty of blogs, and even some free videos that show you are knowledgeable on the topic to the point that visitors are willing to trust you enough to pay for your expert level webinar.

If you have never built a website before, there are plenty of options when it comes to creating something that is functional, if not necessarily flashy. While completely free options are available, you are going to want to invest at least enough in your platform so that you can have your own domain as this will help to build your professional brand. Having an official sounding name will go a long way toward legitimizing your content, which will make it more likely that visitors will be willing to pay for it.

Market your content: Once you have a website that is full of content, both paid and free, the next thing you will want to do is get the word out about your webinar. The first thing you are going to want to do is to spread the word via social media and encourage all of your friends and family to do the same; you never know when something might go viral and word of mouth is enough to boost the sales of a webinar significantly if it gets in front of the right people.

With that out of the way, the next thing you will want to do is visit websites that the people in your chosen niche are likely to congregate around. Once you find these sites you are going to want to spend time in their forums, answering questions that people pose about the topics. Every time you do so, you are then going to want to credit your site as the place you found the information. With enough posts all carrying your website you can be sure that word will start to spread and you will start to see additional hits on your primary site as a result.

Finally, it is important that you include the right type of Search Engine Optimization for your site. This means including the right key phrases as well as a well thought out description to help you show up when people search for the topic you are discussing. The right SEO is extremely important which means that if you don't know what you are doing it is worth paying someone else to do it for you, whatever the cost, you are likely to make it back ten-fold from the extra hits you will receive.

Create an email list: As part of your checkout process, it is important to offer users the ability to sign up for your email list so they can be told when new webinars are available. There is no better audience than one that has already purchased your content, which means whenever you create something new, you will want to send out an email letting these folks know that it is available.

Chapter 8: Author an eBook

If you have detailed knowledge of a particular topic, and want to capitalize on that knowledge without being on camera, then writing an eBook is a valid choice. E-books have been outselling traditional books since 20012 and it is extremely easy to capitalize on this fact and get your piece of the pie. What's more, even if you aren't terribly knowledgeable on a topic, or if your writing skills aren't up to snuff, you can find someone to write a book for you through a surprisingly cheap and easy process.

Get your eBook created: First things first, if you aren't interested in putting together your own eBook, then you can visit a labor sourcing website such as UpWork.com to find easy access to thousands of different writers who are all anxious to complete the task for you. All you have to do is to sign up for a free account and post a listing outlining the basics of what you are looking for and the offers will start flooding in. Then it is simply a matter of finding the writer whose style you like the most and agreeing on the price. Assuming the product you are looking for isn't too complicated the average rate for ghostwriters on UpWork.com is $1 per 100 words, which means you can get an average length eBook for about $100.

Once you have the manuscript in hand, you can then visit Fiverr.com and create a profile before finding someone to format your book for the Kindle Marketplace for $5 and then pay another $5 to have someone create a cover. This means that for less than $120, and no work on your part, you can create something that has the potential to continue generating a profit indefinitely.

Post the book to the Kindle Marketplace: Once you have your book in hand, the next step will be to start making money from it. This is as simple as visiting the Kindle Marketplace and submitting the book, as it doesn't cost you anything to add your book to the marketplace. Instead, Amazon takes a percentage of each eBook that is sold and sends you the rest in the form of a biweekly check. Amazon typically takes 70 percent of the total profit for books that are priced anywhere between $2.99 and $9.99. However, they only take 35 percent of books that are priced below $2.99 and above $9.99. This means that if you price your book at the $1.99 price point you will actually make a greater profit than if you price it at the more common $2.99 price point. What's more, this will also lead to a greater increase in sales, as your book will then be seen as a bargain.

The most common books in the Kindle Marketplace are comprised of the self-help and how-to genres as people who are fans of these genres are always looking for fresh takes on existing problems. Even better, they are condition to always be looking for new ways to solve their problems so just by being new to the Marketplace your book will likely see a boost to its sales.

Find the best topic: If you have already created a webinar then this is a great way to supplement that content. You can then either give your book away for free as a value add for people who purchase your webinar, or even to encourage more people to sign up for your email newsletter. You can also offer it for sale on your website as long as the content differs from what you have already created so that your most diehard fans don't feel cheated by paying for the same content twice.

If you are instead going to have someone else write the book for you, your best bet is to choose a topic that is relatively easy to research, while still not being so simple that those who would be interested in purchasing your book don't just go out and do the research themselves. Additionally, once you find a topic you are interested in pursuing, it is important to visit the Kindle Marketplace and see what the competition is like. While it is virtually impossible to find a topic that hasn't yet been covered in some capacity, you are going to want to try and find one that isn't full of new books that are coming out every week in order to give your book a chance to find an audience.

While you are on the site you are also going to want to take a look at the reviews of the top books in the category to see what people like and, more importantly, what they don' like about what is on display. You can then use these talking points, as a guidepost for the writer to ensure that the content you produce is as likely to find a growing audience as possible.

Regardless if you are writing the book yourself or if you are having someone else do the writing for you it is important to take some time and consider who the target audience of your book is going to be. A book that is written for experts in a field is going to be quite different from one that is written for beginners and having a clear idea of whom the book is for will make narrowing down the correct content to include a much easier task. Writing with the target audience in mind will also make it much easier to ensure your book ends up with plenty of 5-star reviews as well. Positive reviews are crucial, as they will make sure your book is more than just a flash in the pan and help to turn it into a bonified hit.

Ensure your cover is eye catching: When browsing Fiverr.com in order to find the right graphic artist for your cover, it is important to keep in mind that roughly 90 percent of all eBook purchases are based on the cover alone. This means you are going to want to have something that looks profession and eye-catching that stands out from the crowd. When placing your request as for something outside the norm or you are likely to end up with a cover that looks like 9 out of 10 on your chosen topic and your sales will suffer because of it.

Chapter 9: Stock Photos

If you are already familiar with what is required to take a great photo, and you have a way to take photos that is more advanced than your Smartphone, then taking photos and selling them to stock photo websites can be an easy way to generate a steady stream of passive income.

Getting started: There are several major sites that you can apply to if you are interested in pursuing this type of passive income steam including iStockPhoto.com and ShutterStock.com. Each of these sites allows aspiring photographers to post content to their site in exchange for a percentage of the profits when a third party pays to license a picture. These sites generally take between 50 and 85 percent of the profits from each photo with more experienced photographers getting a larger percent of the profits. What this means is that selling stock photos is a numbers game with a quantity of sales being key to success in the long run.

Understand what sells: The first step towards making money through this type of passive income stream is determining what type of photos customers are looking for and understanding how to reproduce the quality that you find. Assuming you are already familiar with the basics of quality photography that means you are going to want to spend some time looking through various categories of photos you are interested in. You will want to find a category that is active enough to make it worth your while to contribute to it, while not being so stuffed with content that it is going to be difficult to get yourself noticed. You will also want to take note of the photos that seemed to be picked the most so that you can get an idea of what types of pictures those who frequent those sites are looking for.

Take some pictures: After you have a clear idea of the types of pictures you are to take, the next step is to get out there and start taking pictures. It was mentioned before, but it bears repeating, if you want to find success in this passive income stream then you are going to want to use something nicer than your Smartphone camera. While those pictures have the potential to be relatively good quality, especially considering where that technology was just a few years ago, if you try and submit Smartphone pictures to these sites there is a very high chance that you will be rejected.

Once you have a number of shots that you feel are of the quality required to get your foot in the door, before you submit them you are going to want to go over them with a fine-toothed comb. To do so you are going to want to blow them up to the largest size possible and keep an eye out for small imperfections that might not otherwise be visible. You never know what size photo customers are going to be looking for and you don't want to lose out on a sale just because something isn't right at the largest size. Besides that, you are always going to want to stick to an exposure rate that is set to 100 percent and to also use a tripod, as blurry pictures are almost never going to be accepted unless the blurriness is obviously done for effect.

Submit the photos: The submission process for the major sites is relatively straightforward, you simply choose a few of your best shots and then send them along to be analyzed by a team of professional who work for the site in question. Once you have been accepted you will need to create a profile. Once you have been given access to post new pictures at your own discretion you will want to ensure that each photo you upload features descriptive text that makes it clear what the photo is of as well as a variety of descriptors that will make it more likely to show up in as many different relevant searches as possible.

You will want to include common keywords as well as those that are outside of the box as your idea will sometimes rub potential customers the right way and they will go for it when they otherwise would have picked something more mainstream. This doesn't mean you are going to want to list your photo in every category possible, however, as doing so is only going to cause people to start ignoring your work, even if it comes up in a category that is actually relevant.

If your work doesn't get accepted to the major sites, you may find success with some of the smaller stock photo sites out there that have much less strict application requirements. As almost anyone can be accepted to these sites, if your work is better than average, but just not quite good enough for the major players then you may even find that these sites work in your favour. What's more, they typically pay a larger cut even to new photographers to make up for the fact that they see a fewer number of customers on average. Remember, stock photos are a numbers game so the more places your photos can be seen by the masses the better.

Promote your photos: When posting your photos to the sites you have been accepted to, it is important to not ignore the free photos section. While posting free photos might seem like a bad way to make money, in reality the opposite is true. If customers aren't ready to pay for a photo quite yet, getting your name in the free section is a good way to get them thinking about your work so that when they are ready to purchase your name is already in their mind. Consider this as an advertising cost and you will likely see more productive hits in the long run.

Chapter 10: Instagram

Instagram is currently seeing more than 400 million users on its site every month and nearly one fourth of those visit the site every single day. With numbers like that it isn't hard to see why advertisers are currently looking to capitalize on content creators that have a significant following. While starting an Instagram page now isn't exactly getting in on the ground floor, when it comes to passive income streams it can still be a profitable and fairly open market.

Determine your focus: In order to build the type of audience that advertisers are looking for, the first thing you are going to need to do is focus on generating a loyal following, with the more followers the better. The greater the number of followers you have, the more you will ultimately be able to make via advertising. A good number to shoot for is 20,000 followers before you start reaching out to advertisers and if you reach 100,000 followers then you can currently expect to make anywhere from $5,000 to $10,000 each month in advertising revenue.

The easiest way to start building your number of followers is to add the right types of details to your profile. Information about yourself and the content you post is a good place to start but you are going to want to include plenty more as well. Specifically, you are going to want to include relevant keywords along with popular hashtags as that will help those interested in your chosen niche find you more easily which means you won't just be posting pictures into the ether. It is important that you choose a niche that you are going to remain interested in for a prolonged period of time. If you have a topic in mind but feel you will be bored of it within six months or less it is best to go back to the drawing board as succeeding in this market means interacting with your chosen niche every single day.

Find the right details: In order to ensure you are using keywords and hashtags that are popular, and thus potentially profitable, the first thing you are going to want to do is search Instagram and see how many other users are using the same ones. You aren't going to simply want to use, as may keywords as possible, as this won't get you any new followers, instead you are going to want to stick to those that are actually relevant to the types of pictures you are actually taking. Careful curation is key to attracting niche followers while also not showing up so frequently that searchers consider your page as spam.

Post every single day: Once you have an idea of the type of content you are going to regularly post, it is important to get into the habit of posting multiple times per day, every single day. You will want to find a schedule of posting that you can stick with long enough that potential followers get used to visiting your page every single day and checking in multiple times as well. Once they realize they are visiting your page this often then they will take the plunge and become your followers rather than having to track your page down manually.

It is important to keep in mind that this will only work if you are taking the types of pictures that people are legitimately interested in seeing. If you don't naturally take lots of pictures then you are probably better off pursuing a different passive income stream.

Taking the right types of pictures: In order to determine what types of pictures your potential followers are going to be interested in, you are going to want to visit the pages of plenty of popular individuals in your chosen niche. This doesn't mean you are going to simply want to copy what you find there, however, but instead you are going to want to use what you find as inspiration. This will help get your creative juices flowing and make it easier to come up with content of your own in the future. Developing your own unique perspective is crucial to being successful in the long run.

While you are on these pages, you are going to want to do more than simply lurk, instead you are going to want to post comments on pictures you like and start interacting with the community. After all, running a successful Instagram isn't just about posting photos, it is about being a personality. Then, once people associated with the niche find your page, you won't be just another random person you will be another member of the community.

Tag individual photos: Once you have taken plenty of pictures that you think the community will enjoy, it is important to go ahead and post them using the keywords and hashtags that you find other people using. Additionally, you are going to want to develop your own keyword or hashtag that your followers can associate with all of your pictures. This will help make it easier for them to keep track of all your new posts.

Turn a profit: Once you have built up a sizeable following, you can start strengthening your passive income stream. The easiest way to go about doing so is by posting pictures of you with niche specific products and then including a link to those products and explaining where people can purchase them. The Amazon affiliate program is great for this, but only if you don't abuse it. If your page suddenly changes from niche specific photos to nothing but affiliate marketing then your follower count will suffer as a result. Instead, you are going to want to work these types of pictures into your content stream naturally.

Also, you are going to want to look into advertisers that work via the pay per click model. Essentially how it works is that you offer advertising space on your page and then receive a small amount of compensation each time one of your followers clicks on the ad, regardless of what they do after they have done so. While the average rate for this type of advertisement is just a few cents per click, with at least 20,000 followers this can still add up rather quickly. Additionally, you can look for advertisers who pay per impression, which means you get paid every time a follower visits your page, regardless of whether or not they click on anything. The rate for these types of ads is even less than the pay per click model, but a combination of both can be a profitable venture.

Conclusion

Thank you for making it through to the end of Passive Income Stream Generator: Top 10 Ways to Financial Freedom, let's hope it was informative and able to provide you with all of the tools you need to achieve your goals, whatever it is that they may be. Just because you've finished this book doesn't mean there is nothing left to learn on the topic, expanding your horizons is the only way to find the mastery you seek. New types of passive income streams are always being discovered and the only way you will stay on top of them is by doing your own research.

As you can see, there are plenty of different ways to generate passive income, but getting them up and running requires hard work and dedication before you can sit back and reap the rewards from all of your hard work. This means you are going to want to pick one of the types of passive income discussed in the previous chapters and dedicate yourself to it until it starts turning a profit. Flitting from one type of passive income stream to the next will only end up burning you out on the process as a whole without generating any real revenue in the process.

When you are in the midst of setting up a passive income stream it can be easy to lose sight of the end goal amidst the hard work. It is important to stay the course, however, and to keep in mind that the ends are certainly going to justify the means. You don't need anything special in order to set up a successful passive income stream, you just need to commit yourself to the process and see it through to completion. Remember, generating passive income is a marathon, not a sprint; slow and steady wins the race.

Finally, if you found this book useful in anyway, a review on Amazon is always appreciated!

Rental Property Investing

A Step-by-Step Guide to Getting Your First Real Estate Property

Table of Contents

Introduction 60

Chapter 1: About Real Estate 61

Chapter 2: Beginning Your Journey 71

Chapter 3: Renovating and Getting Move in Ready 94

Chapter 4: Picking the Right Tenants 110

Chapter 5: Becoming a Landlord 113

Chapter 6: Do's and Don'ts 118

Chapter 7: Extra Tips for Maximizing Profit 130

Conclusion 143

Copyright 2017 - All rights reserved.

This document is geared towards providing exact and reliable information in regards to the topic and issue covered. The publication is sold on the idea that the publisher is not required to render an accounting, officially permitted, or otherwise, qualified services. If advice is necessary, legal or professional, a practiced individual in the profession should be ordered.

- From a Declaration of Principles which was accepted and approved equally by a Committee of the American Bar Association and a Committee of Publishers and Associations.

In no way is it legal to reproduce, duplicate, or transmit any part of this document by either electronic means or in printed format. Recording of this publication is strictly prohibited, and any storage of this document is not allowed unless with written permission from the publisher. All rights reserved.

The information provided herein is stated to be truthful and consistent, in that any liability, in terms of inattention or otherwise, by any usage or abuse of any policies, processes, or directions contained within is the solitary and utter responsibility of the recipient reader. Under no circumstances will any legal responsibility or blame be held against the publisher for any reparation, damages, or monetary loss due to the information herein, either directly or indirectly.

Respective authors own all copyrights not held by the publisher.

Introduction

Thank you for purchasing this book. If you are looking to engage in the real estate world, this is the book for you. You will learn how to make money, and make your money work for you.

If you are looking to expand your mind in all things real estate, specifically how to start the process, this is the book for you. You will learn more about how to start out in an industry that most people don't even think about as a financial option.

These days, the housing market is ripe for the picking, and the profits are fairly impressive. Get out there, and find the financial freedom that you desire.

Enjoy and best of luck.

Chapter 1: About Real Estate

It seems that you are interested in this fast paced world. However, before you begin, you have to know exactly what real estate investing is, and what all goes into the process. You really have to be sure that you are prepared for this specific industry, because if you are not properly prepared, then you might need to spend a little more time getting ready. This is an industry that can make you rich, but it can also cause some serious financial drain if you are not ready for the whole ordeal.

This book is here to help you as you embark on the adventure of real estate investing. When you try to go out into the world, you feel like you are alone most of the time. This book will help you feel less alone and misguided by giving you the information that you need to get through each day with more and more progress. When you are trying to start your journey into the world of real estate, the beginner level is actually the most difficult. You have so much to learn, and you have to do well the first time especially because it is the precursor of your potential in the investment.

This industry is a lot different than a lot of other investing platforms. It is not as cutthroat, but it is still a make it or break it kind of deal. It also can take a good chunk of change to start up. It all depends on your area and what kind of deals that you can find. If you know where to look, then you can definitely ensure that you can get the best deals out there, just keep your eyes open.

I know what you are thinking: "You haven't yet got around to telling me what exactly real estate investing is." And you are exactly right. However, I am getting there now, just needed to prepare you so that you know that even though it sounds easy, and it can be easy, it does take time and effort, along with money.

Real estate investing is the process of buying a house for as low of a price as you can get it, fixing it up and adding value to it, and either selling the house for a profit or renting it out for a steadier income. This book is going to mainly focus on the second option because it is the best investment strategy out there. When you are renting a property, you become a landlord, and the people who rent from you are known as tenants. You, as the landlord, have a steady income coming in, while your tenants have a nice place to live where they don't have to pay property taxes or deal with registering a deed.

This is different from the other ways of investing because no other investment platform allows you to earn a steady income, and make as much profit as you can with renting. If you are smart with your money, you can make almost a 75% return on your investment over a period of time. However, investing in real estate does often take longer to build up to where you make it past breaking even. With other investments, it may take some time to see a return, but with real estate investing, it can take a few years. Also, with real estate investing, you do not have to sell your investment to start making money. You can keep your investment and still make money off of it. That is the greatest thing about this platform. Then, when you are tired of being the one responsible for it, and you have made more money than you could have imagined off of your investment, you can sell it, which could even give you more money than your profit you made on the house renting it did if inflation has occurred in the market. There are so many pros in this industry that many people often overlook the cons. Let us weigh both shall we?

Pros

There are many pros in this industry. That is what makes it so desirable. These pros could be the reasons that you decide you want to invest in real estate, so let's look at them all.

- Steady: Most investments are not very steady. Once you get the money, you have to reinvest it to make any more money. Real estate has the ability to make you continual money with minimal reinvestment. You can also get your money almost immediately, rather than having to sit on an investment for months and years on end to make any profit from the investment. Having a steady income can make this more than a hobby; it can make it a wonderful opportunity for your financial gain.

- Money: You can make more money in this business than you can in most types of investments unless you pick a lucky stock. This means that with real estate investing, you can really start to live your life the way you dreamed once the money starts rolling in.

- More Hands On: This is only a pro for some, but it is still a pro. You can be active on your investment, and you call all the shots. This means that if you have a problem with your investment not making money, you can find out why and fix it right away.

- Safer: This industry is a lot safer than most investment markets because you don't have to worry about a sudden market crash. There are always going to be people who need a place to live, and are not able to buy a house for whatever reason, or they do not want to buy a house just yet. So there are always going to be someone who needs to rent.

Cons

There are some cons in this industry as well. It is important that you know about them because you do not want to get blindsided by one. While there are not many cons, they may be the reason you decide you do not want to be a part of this industry, so it is better to know about them before you have already invested your money.

- Money: It takes this investment platform longer to build up money than the other ones. You have to have patience with it, and be able to keep money incoming from other sources. The less you have to spend in the beginning, the sooner the actual profit will start rolling in.

- Not Constant: The steady income does come at a price. You have to continually make sure that there is a paying person in your property. Otherwise the money you have come to depend on halts suddenly. You have to work hard to keep your rentals and your properties continually in use so that you have continual money. This can be a struggle in the current financial market.

- More Hands On: This is also a con for some people. There are people out there that don't want to be in control of everything, because then when something goes wrong, it is for them to fix it. That is the case here. If something breaks and it was part of what you provided upon moving in, you are required to fix or replace it.

These are the cons that you will definitely have to think about when deciding on if you want to join the business of real estate investing. If you can live with the fact that this is not a dream moneymaking ordeal, then you may find that in time you make the money you need and more.

If you are asking yourself the question: "Why should I invest in real estate?" You again have come to the right book to get your answer. This would not be a book for beginners if we did not answer that question, or at least give you a little more clarity, so here are some reasons why you should invest in real estate.

- Be Your Own Boss: No one can tell you what to do. You call the shots, and you make the decisions. You can decide what color to paint the walls. You can decide which property you want to buy, and how to price it. You work on your own schedule and answer to no one but yourself. It is freeing and very enticing to have

Passive Income Stream Generator

that sort of freedom.

- Financial Freedom: Once you get established, and start making a profit, you will be relieved at the financial freedoms that you find yourself enjoying. This is one of the main reasons to become a real estate investor. Imagine being able to take a vacation with your family, and not have to pinch pennies the entire time. Imagine being able to do what everyone wants, so you don't have to see any disappointed faces. How many times have you gone on a family vacation, and one kid wanted to do something that was just too expensive for you to afford? How much did it kill you to tell that kid it just wasn't in the cards to go? With the financial freedom to go do those things, you can take back your life, and you can take back the fun.

- Beating the Odds: So many people are skeptics that they make up statistics of failure to justify telling someone it can't be done, and discouraging them when in reality they are just jealous that they don't have the ability to do so. They don't feel like sticking their neck out, so they miss the chance to succeed, and they think that other people shouldn't try either. Succeed to make them even more jealous, but also succeed to inspire them.

- Tangible Investments: If you own stocks in a company, it is less thrilling to drive by the building and say "I own a half a percent of that building" than it is to drive by your investment properties and say, "I own that." This makes it a lot easier for people to see your success as well, just be sure not to brag too much.

These are just some of the reasons for you to invest. There are many more reasons out there, but some are more specific than others, so only the basic ones are listed. Try it for yourself to see why it is such a great idea.

Now that you know what real estate investing is, the pros and cons, and why you should invest, if you are still reading, I assume that you want to continue on your journey. Now we give you the tips and tricks for becoming a success. These tips and tricks will help figure out what it is that you need to do, and how to make it big.

Chapter 2: Beginning Your Journey

The tips in this chapter are what you need to know to start out before you even make your first purchase. These tips will walk you through how to plan a budget and how to look for the perfect house without being blinded by the cosmetics of the house. You will learn how to look past the surface, and how to decide if you have found the right property or if you need to keep moving.

This chapter is essential to your success. If you do not start out on the right foot, it can be all downhill from there. You want to have a solid foundation to build an investment empire in which to free yourself from everyday financial burdens. You have to make sure that you are doing what it takes to ensure success.

Budget

The first thing that you have to make sure that you

have sorted out is your budget. This means that you have to know exactly how much money you are going to have to begin with. It is essential that you make sure you know exactly how much money you want to spend before you start looking for a property, so you do not run the risk of overspending.

However, you cannot just know how much you have to spend because budgeting goes way deeper than that. You have to set aside money to do a multitude of things. So even if you got a loan for $80,000, you still would not be able to go out and buy n $80,000 house. You have to make sure that you have money left over to do other things.

For example, you need money set aside to do any necessary renovations. These may or may not be extensive. If you go and you buy a house for $80,000, and you find out it needs new water lines, where are you going to get the money? You have to dig into your pockets even more, and if you don't have the funds at the ready, that halts your money making process, and that is not a good thing.

You also have to be sure that you are able to cover closing costs because those will get you every time. What people don't tell you is that you often are the one paying the real estate agents fees and filing for all of the paperwork. It all falls on you. Plus, you also have to pay the down payment for the loan, which comes out of your pocket. This means that you have to be prepared and have the money set aside to buy a property.

There aren't just renovations and closing costs that you have to think about. You also have to take in consideration that you have to prepare for property taxes, and the property being empty for a time. Filing fees if you have a lawyer draw up your contracts for renters. There are a lot of little expenses that you have to take into account before you set aside your budget for buying a house. Otherwise, you will find yourself running out of money pretty quickly.

If you have an $80,000 loan, you do not really have to spend it all on the house. The best way to budget is to try to stay around half to three-quarters of what you have when you are looking for a house. Though realistically you will not be able to get a loan that big unless you have superb credit, and even if you could, as a first-time rental investor, it is best to stay around $40,000 unless you are in a really expensive area.

In some areas, $40,000 is plenty of money to find a

good rental property investment- especially if you live in a less populated town. In a more populated town, you may have to get a bigger loan. However, we will stick with the Midwest figures for now just so you get a general idea of how to portion up your money.

Say you go to the bank. Your credit is decent, but not stellar, and you don't want to pay more than three hundred a month on your mortgage so that you can still make a profit from your rental. The bank offers you a $40,000 loan, with only a $5,000 down payment. You say that is perfect because all you have to put down on loan is $6,000 and you also wanted money to pay the first-month payment on the loan.

So now you are planning on looking for a house. You have to figure out exactly how much you have to spend on said house, and still have some money left over to make changes to it, and prepare it for a rental property. That means that you should try to find a house between $20,000 and $27,000. You may think that you can't find something that affordable, and you won't find a six bedroom perfectly updated 5,000-square foot mansion. However, you could find a two- to three-bedroom house with a nice yard in a quiet neighborhood. It may need work, but you shouldn't have to put too much work into it to make it a nice place.

So after that, you should plan to put around $6,000 to $8,000 into place, to make it look nice. It may need less than that, however, if it needs more, you should move on (Always find out how much you need to renovate before closing). After spending that much, you have about $4,000 to $6,000 on the low end left after all that.

That money is to cover closing costs, the cost of hiring and inspector, and other general necessities for the house that you will need before you rent it out. After you have finished all of that, you may have at max a thousand dollars left. You should put this money into an emergency fund for the property. That is what you will need if something happens to the house. (You should add to that money on a regular basis, but that will be discussed later)

This is how you budget your money well and make sure that you are not going to overspend on buying a property and be up a creek with no paddle. You have to have the finances to get this process moving as quickly as you possibly can, because time is money, and in investing, money is everything.

Searching for the Right Property

The first thing that you should remember is that you are not looking for a forever home for yourself. You are looking for an investment property that may see a lot of different people living in it and will need to be repaired a lot. So you do not want to find a high-end house with all the fancy furnishings. You want to find a house that looks nice, but also fits the bill for what you need it for.

It is important that you follow the steps in this tip group because you want to find a house that is not going to be a money pit. Otherwise, you are going to be really in for it in the long run. You want to find a house that even though it may need a little bit of work, does not need to be completely redone- unless you bought it for really cheap. The tips in this section will help you find that property, and will show you the buying markets that are out there, and rank them on which is the best for a new investor, and which is not the best for a new investor, but can still turn up a few gold mines.

The tips will also walk you through the buying process, and help you find what to look for when you actually do the walk through the process to find a good house. You want to be sure you find the right house before you sign on the line and become stuck with your investment no matter how good or bad it may be.

The first thing you have to know though is where to look for a house. This is important because you want to find a good deal, that isn't going to leave you high and dry in the end. Remember some good deals are snakes in disguise, so you want to use caution and your head when you are looking to buy.

- Real Estate Agency: This is by far the safest way to go. You will have someone there to guide you, and his or her goal is to ensure that you are satisfied and that you have found the right house for you. They will walk you through finding what you need. However, they don't get paid if they don't sell a house, so there is always more pressure to buy when you are not sure if you are quite ready to buy. This is not really a big deal, as they do not force you to buy, and they truly do want you to find a great house, but you also have to remember, the realtor has to look out for their bottom line as well.

- Classifieds: There is nothing better than an old-fashioned classified ad when you are looking for something. These are pretty safe because they pay to put the ad in the paper, and most people would not do so if they didn't think their property was worth it. You often can make your own times to check out a house without having to go through a realtor. This means that if you decide not to buy it, you won't have to deal with any guilt about taking up even more time. With classified ads, you have to be careful though. Sometimes there are people who pay to take an ad out, but the house is not worth it.

- Online: This one is kind of 50-50. You can find a gem, or you could find a flop. You have to approach this one with caution, and you have to make sure that you are cautious when going to see a house from someone off the Internet. Take a friend or two with you. Never go alone. Not everyone is a psycho out to get you, but there are a few. In fact, any time you are going to look at a property without a realtor, it is always best to go in pairs. There is always safety in numbers.

How to find a house online is the real question? Many people post their houses in Facebook Groups. Do a search for sale groups/for rent in your area, and you should find several. This is a safer way to look for houses because there are several people that know about the house, and the person who posted it. You can set up the time, and if things don't go as expected, then you can warn others as well. There is also Craigslist. This is known as the seedier version of a classified ad, but there are still good houses on there. Craigslist honestly gets a bad reputation. As long as you use common sense, then you will be fine.

- Auctions: These are really useful if you have a good amount of money for remodeling, but you want to get a house really low priced. Housing auctions happen when someone doesn't know how to price a property or doesn't want to spend a long time getting it sold. Generally, these properties are run down, but you may be able to get a gem if you are lucky. However, be careful, banks often auction off unsold foreclosures that have high property taxes on them. If you are alerted to the property before it goes up for auction, check into the property taxes on it. If not, you are taking a risk, and hopefully, you get the house for cheap enough to cover all of the costs of the house.

- Foreclosures: These are really desirable in their pricing, but they can be snakes in disguise. Foreclosures are when a bank has taken back a house that somebody quit paying the mortgage on. They often put it back on the market for how much is left on the note. This means if the person paid it off quite a bit, the house could be fairly cheap. This will draw you in, but you have to use caution.

These houses can be snakes in disguise. They often have a lot of back taxes that are owed on them. If the house is not reasonably priced enough to cover the difference, then you should walk away as fast as you can because the taxes are what will get you.

Once you have decided how you want to go about finding a house, you can start your search. There are some things that you should keep in mind when searching for a house.

First off, take a look at the neighborhood. Is it a safe one? Not many people want to live in a neighborhood that is known for drug or gang activity, so make sure that the property you are looking at is in a nicer neighborhood. In a school zone is ideal because those are the most desirable houses for families with children who are established enough to afford a house in that area. This means that you are almost guaranteed to have people in your property fairly quickly. Check the rating of the school. The higher the rating, the higher you can price the rent.

Also, you have to learn the average rent prices in the area. You want to stay within the confines of comparable house rent prices because if you are too high, people will be turned off from your property. If you can keep within the confines of the general rent, and still make a profit, then the property is good to go, however, if you cannot, then you should probably look elsewhere.

You have to look at the house itself as well. Is it in decent condition, does it look like it needs a lot of repairs, will it be costly? This doesn't mean the ugly color of paint on the wall. This means does it look like it has evidence of leaks, infestations, and other issues. The best way to figure this out is to have the property inspected. You should save an inspection for the property you really want to buy, though, because they can get costly. For the first walk through, just use your own eyes, and see if you can spot anything that could be a problem later on.

Look into the back taxes, and how much they cost. Also, check how much it would the monthly utility bill be. If they are high, it could be an indication that there is a problem somewhere that needs to be addressed immediately. If the taxes and utilities are high, it may be a good idea to just go on to a different property. Because you do not want to be stuck with a property that is going to sit empty or be a money drain.

If the property you are looking at passes all of the tests, then you can go on to making an offer, and hopefully close the deal on it. There are a few tips for going to make an offer, so as to ensure that you have a good shot at getting the house.

Rules for Finding a House

- **Don't look for a home. Look for a house.**

The truth is you're not looking for something that you could see yourself living in. You are looking for something to make a profit. A lot of people pass up a good investment opportunity because they "can't see themselves in the house, and wouldn't want to market it." However, you could make the house better with just a little work. You are not looking for a move-in ready house that suits you, you are looking for a house you can make a decent profit off of.

- **Don't let your emotions rule you.**

Your emotions can get in the way of your logical mind when it comes to purchasing. Perhaps you have found the perfect house, but you won't get a lot of profit. Maybe you found a house that seems like a steal but has more problems than it is worth. If you let your emotions get in the way, you can seriously cause an issue with your bottom line. You have to keep your emotions out of business, and that is what this is. No matter how quaint or perfect a house is, if it is not good for profit, you have to walk away. No matter how good a deal may seem, if you find it is not worth it, don't forge on with the deal. It may seem simple, but emotions are tricky in the simplest places.

- **Don't be afraid of auctions.**

Too many people want to buy outright. They do not want to go to an auction and sit and bid on properties. There are a lot of stigmas about auction properties being duds anyways, when a lot of times, you can get a property for really cheap, and even after paying any back taxes, you are still way under budget. For people who want to rent out houses, it doesn't really matter, but for flippers like you, an auction can be a gold mine.

- **Ugly is money**

This is a phrase that you should take to heart. A house may look ugly, but as long as the structure is sound, and everything is to code, you will find that you can make a great profit with an ugly house. All it takes is a little paint and updating, and the house you bought for under market value goes up in value at least one margin. This is flipping at its finest.

- **Don't Settle.**

There are so many options out there. Don't settle for the first deal you can find. Pick out several options and then narrow it down from there. You have to find what is best for you and your pocketbook. Too many people get the itch that they have to start flipping immediately, so they take the first cheap house that they can find without doing any research. Take your time and look into every option carefully. Eventually, you can make hastier decisions after you have established a profit base, and have more knowledge in the field. For now, especially for your first house purchase, you have to be careful.

- Negotiate, but Be Reasonable: It is always okay to offer a little less than what the seller is asking, but you have to use common sense. No one wants to be low-balled when they are trying to sell something, so don't offer $10,000 on a $20,000 house. Eighteen or nineteen is about as low as you should go, depending on how firm they are on the price.

- Don't Jump: A lot of people are too scared to push the envelope when it comes to the negotiation process, so they take the first counter offer that they get from the sellers. However, you often can talk them down closer to your number than their original number if you show you are willing to come up a bit. However, people are scared to anger the seller and lose their chance at getting the house altogether. There is a key to knowing when to jump and when to hold out for more.

It all has to do with the timing. You have to pay attention to how quickly they counter. If they counter pretty quickly, then you have a good chance at getting it closer to your number. However, if they respond really slowly with a counter, and if you are able to afford what they are counting reasonably, then it would be best to take it. Also, pay attention to how much they come down from their price to see how much you need to come up. If they come down a little, you should come up a little. If they come down a lot, be willing to go up some more to find a compromise.

- Don't Make Threats: A lot of movies and television shows portray a person threatening to walk over a minute difference in their numbers when buying a house, and the sellers contact them with an offer they can't refuse. This is not how it works in the real world. More often than not, a seller will let you walk, so they have a better chance at selling the house closer to their desired number. The seller does not have to play chase, and most will not even attempt to pursue you when they know that they have the upper hand.

- Ask to Split Closing: In your offer, you should always ask for the seller to split closing costs, so they do not all fall on you. Closing costs can get expensive, after paying the realtor and filing all of the paperwork with the right departments. Most sellers are prepared to help with closing and have an escrow set aside to do so. If you are lucky, some sellers will cover closing if you settle on a number that is closer to their asking price.

Extra Tips for Making a Good Buy or Sale

- ### What to Do When You Find a House

So you think you have found the perfect house? Well, there are still a lot of things to do before you close the deal. The only exception is with an auction house. You have to do some of these things before the auction. So this section will be broken down into two parts: A regular sale/foreclosure sale and auction houses.

- ### Regular Sales

When you find a house that is being sold, there are a few steps you have to take. Whether the house is being sold through an agency, direct through the seller, or a foreclosure, you have to do some background checks on the house. Everything that you need to know is public knowledge, so you don't have to worry about paying an arm and a leg when you are looking into these things.

The first thing that you have to look into is the neighborhood. How does the neighborhood look? Is it clean and well kept? If so, that is a good mark for the house. If not, that is a mark against it. Two marks against a house and you should move on. The look of a neighborhood is very important when it comes to profit. People are more likely to buy a house in a neighborhood that is clean and nice looking. If neighbors have broken down cars all over their yards, and grass that is really tall, or houses that are just in shambles, then you will have a harder time selling the house.

The next thing that you have to look into is the crime rate in the neighborhood. This is one of those things that is super important to look into. If the crime rate is too high, even if everything else seems okay, then you should probably move on to a different area. No one wants to live in a neighborhood where there are going to be sirens every other day. They also don't want to live in fear that they are going to get robbed every time they turn around.

School districts are pretty important as well. Make sure that the location is in a school district that has a good rating. The better the school rating the more desirable the location. You will draw in young families who want their kids to have a good education, and the better the school district, the more you can sell the house for. Which is great if you find one that needs work, causing it to be really cheap, and you fix it up well. Profit will swim your way with haste.

Back taxes- the nastiest word in this business. To properly sell a house, it is best to pay up the back taxes on it. A lot of houses don't have back taxes, but especially in the case of a foreclosure, you can never be too sure. You always have to do a check. It is a simple thing to do. Just call the local city office, and they will tell you if there are taxes owed on the property, and how much they total up to.

Once you have looked into all of these things, you should get the property inspected. This does not happen until you are talking deals, but it should happen before you close and shake on anything. An inspection can alert you to anything that is wrong with the property that may not be visible to an untrained eye.

- **Auction Houses**

When you first start out, it is best to go to a visible auction. These are auctions where you are alerted to the property ahead of time and have a chance to check it out. With these auctions, pretty much everything is the same, except you may not be able to get it inspected unless you have a friend that is an inspector with you when they allow you to walk through the property.

With a blind auction, you do not get to see the property; most times you do not even get the address until the auction. This is where having a phone with data is important. As soon as you get the address, pull it up on Google maps so that you can check out the house, and the neighborhood. It will give you an idea as to if the house is worth it or not. Pull up any specs on the property that you can. You have to be quick so that you can start bidding. It is best to go to these auctions when you are more advanced in the process.

- **Avoiding a Mishap**

There is no secret that buying a house can be tricky. What seems like a great property can really cause you a lot of headaches. You have to be aware of the warning signs when you are looking into a property.

- **#1 Pushy Seller**

The first warning sign of a problem is a pushy seller. Generally, these sellers will get agitated when you ask any questions about the property, and they would prefer you to just buy the house without doing any research. They may be insulted that you want to check into back taxes or have an inspection on the house. If you run into a pushy seller, it is best to turn tail and run.

- **#2 Ramshackle Neighborhood**

As stated above, a ramshackle neighborhood is already a mark against the property. However, it goes deeper than just aesthetic. If a property resides in one of these neighborhoods, generally the property itself will have problems, because there will be no competition to make the property look nice, and to keep up with the maintenance.

- **#3 Weak Handshake/No Handshake**

It is a fact that a weak handshake or a lack of handshake should set off alarm bells. Handshakes help you judge whether a person is trustworthy or not. If they don't shake your hand, or barely touch you when they do, then the seller probably has something to hide. This may be followed by lack of eye contact as well. Body language is the best warning sign there is.

If you watch for the signs of a bad property, you should be able to avoid the problems that come with a bad property.

Those are the tips to successfully negotiating the buying of your first investment property. Once you have obtained the property, it is time to move on to renovations.

Chapter 3: Renovating and Getting Move in Ready

Once you have bought your first investment property, you then have to renovate and get the property ready for people to move in. This means that you are going to have to do some planning. You always have to have a plan after you buy a house to make a time frame for getting the house on the market and rented out. To make the plan you must first establish what needs to be done to the house, and then decide if you are doing the renovations yourself. (Not recommended if you have no experience unless only cosmetic things need to be done.) You also have to decide what can stay and what can go in the house. That allows for a time difference as well.

Once you have a plan set in place, it is time to start the renovations. There are some tips for how to go about renovating, and how to save money in order to ensure that you can have a nice emergency fund set aside.

Renovating

When renovating your house, there are a few things that you should know. These tips will help you save money, while still delivering a quality rental in the end. Just because you saved money, does not mean you are "cheap," it means that you are smart, so long as you made sure to spend money where it was needed. These tips will not only help you save money but will also help you distinguish between saving money and being cheap.

- If it Works: If it works, leave it! If you do not need to replace something, then you should not. You are not making a dream home for yourself, you are making a house for others to live in. It needs to be functional, and look decent. That means if the house came with appliances, but they are not the newest ones, leave them. If the tenants want to use their own, then they can. If the cabinets are in good condition, leave them. Try giving them a coat of paint if you don't like the way they look.

- Clean: Sometimes, a house is in such good condition, that all it needs is a good cleaning. More than the seller did. Polish the wood, shine the glass, and make it look shiny and new. If it has carpet that is fairly new, just have it deep cleaned. (Unless previous owners had pets. Then it has to be replaced.) You would be surprised at how nice things look with just a little finessing and elbow grease. Of course, most first time investments need a little bit of work, but if you are lucky enough to find one that just needs to be cleaned, then you are best to leave it at that, and save your renovation money for an emergency fund.

- Alternative materials: These are great! Linoleums have come a long way than the green and white ugly kitchen floors of the seventies. Now almost every textile has a laminate copy. This is a great thing, because linoleum is affordable, and if it gets damaged, it does not cost an arm and a leg to get fixed. It is also pretty durable, so it can withstand a lot. There are a lot of other alternative materials out there as well, that look like high-end products, without the high-end price tag. This means that you can get a good product fairly affordable.

- Reuse: If you want to replace something, try to use it elsewhere in the house. Like, say you want to put a better bathtub in the master bathroom to really separate it as the master bath, use the current working tub in the guest bathroom if it only has a shower. (As long as there is space). Anything that you can reuse, then you should try your best to put it to use. Waste costs money. And if you lose money in waste, that is literally money in the trash. In this industry, money is the goal, and the more you lose, the further you are in your goal.

- Garage sales: Not everything bought from a garage sale is cheap. There are often a lot of quality items that are found at garage sales if you are looking hard enough. A lot of people are only selling the stuff because they don't need it anymore. Especially in country club areas. And a lot of stuff the country club people just give away, because they don't need it anymore and were just going to throw it away anyway. Just be careful to be sure not to invite pest infestations in your own home. Checking the item over with a flashlight should prove to show you if it is clean or not.

- Only DIY Where You Can: It is the general consensus that if you do everything yourself. This is not necessarily the case. If you know how to do something, then by all means, save yourself the money. But only if you really know how to do it, and have successfully done it before. Otherwise, you could be in for a heap of trouble. Knowing how to do something does not refer to watching a video online, and then saying that you are an expert. If you are going to do it that way, take out a thousand dollars, and throw it in the trash right now. Because that is essentially what you are doing when you do this. Except in cosmetic cases where anyone can do those, if you are trying to do everything DIY and you have no experience at all, then you are running a high risk of making things worse, rather than better. An expert may cost more upfront, but in the long run will save you money, because, with a repairman, it will last a long time and truly fix the problem, not cause a bigger problem later on.

However, if you do know how to do something, do it. Don't spend money on something you can save it on. Your goal is to be able to make a profit as soon as you possibly can, and the more you spend on startup, the longer it will take to make that money back. If you know how to fix a busted pipe, don't hire a plumber. If you know how to change an outlet, and fix faulty wiring, don't hire an electrician. When you hire someone, they charge you for as much as they can charge you without being a scam artist. They charge you for having to travel to the location, for the parts they use, for their time, and for their labor. This is a very important thing to remember because a lot of people want their rentals to be professionally worked over, and then they wonder why it cost so much to get the work done. It is because these people are trying to run a business, and you don't make any money if you are only making what you put in. You have to do what you can to keep the costs low and be able to still deliver a quality house to your potential renters.

- Friends are Essential: If you have a few good buddies, enlist their help to get the job done. It is cheaper to pay your friends than it is to pay professionals, and you will save money in the long run, because even though you are paying other people, you will have the house ready to rent out sooner, which means less time that you are paying on the mortgage yourself, and the sooner you can start making a profit.

These are some tips to help you through the renovation process. Avoid big box stores. They deliver below quality products for a high price. Liquidation outlets and other low-priced stores are the best way to go. You can get quality products for a low price. Liquidation outlets buy overstock from companies or things that were going to just be thrown out due to damaged packaging, despite the fact the product was still in good condition. This means savings for you because they can pass those low prices down. The product is often some pretty good stuff as well. So you don't have to worry about your rental being a basic "cheap" looking place.

Speaking of cheap. There is a huge difference between affordable and cheap. Cheap is when you don't fix something because it is "not that bad" and you don't want to spend the money on it. And then when it completely breaks after a tenant moves in, you try to put that on the tenant to pay. Cheap is also buying the lowest quality things that you can find because they are the absolute cheapest without caring how it will hold up. Being cheap actually gets rather expensive. However, buying affordable products does not make you cheap, as long as the product is still of decent quality. If you make sure that everything that needs to be fixed is fixed properly, and you still put quality products on your property, no matter the low price, you are not cheap.

You want your property to be comfortable and inviting. However, if you put really expensive products into your rental, and you spend a lot of money on renovations, you will never make money because you will have to constantly fix or replace them. Tenants live under the pretense that if it breaks, they are not responsible because, by law, it is the landlord's responsibility to take care of the property and replace something that breaks. Unless it is in the contract otherwise, you have to replace anything that is damaged. Since the tenants do not feel responsible for the property, they are more likely to not treat it with care than they would be if they were the owner of the house. This is why you charge a deposit on the move in, to ensure that when they move out, you can fix any damage, but if you have high-end products in your home, the deposit is not going to cover an entire overhaul. However, if you have affordable products in your home, it is a lot less expensive to replace the materials that are damaged. You want to be able to save as much money as you can to put in an emergency fund so that you are not digging into your profits if something goes wrong with something on the property, such as a sewer line rupture, or something to that effect. Or even little things, like a robber busting the window or the door jam. You want to be able to make the needed repairs without having to worry where the money comes from. However, we will talk more about emergency funds and how to create one later on.

Now it is time to move on to staging and getting the property ready to show. These tips are important for making your property look like a potential home, rather than just a house.

Staging

This is something that a lot of rental property owners try to skip because they feel that it is too expensive to do, and they do not want to shell out that type of cash. However, staging does not have to be expensive, and you need to stage your home. Otherwise, you are going to have a property that sits empty for longer than you wish. Houses sell thirty percent faster with even just basic staging.

Staging is important, because it shows the potential tenants what the house is really like, and shows them with a reference if they are able to fit in the house reasonably. A lot of houses look really roomy when they are empty. However, most people know this, and so they shrink it in their mind to the point where they won't think they will fit well. With staging, they can get an accurate representation of the true size of the house.

Staging does not have to be elaborate, and you don't have to have perfect matching furniture, and a full sectional couch in the living room, along with a thousand-dollar bedroom set in the master bedroom, you just have to show people what the room size is like. There are a few affordable options for staging a home, and they all depend on if you are furnishing the house, or if you are just staging it to show it.

If you are going to stage the house just to show it, then you are in luck. This is the most affordable thing to do because there is such a thing as cardboard furniture. This is a great resource, because it is very low cost to do, and pretty easy to make as well. Cardboard furniture is exactly what it implies. Furniture made from cardboard.

To create it, all you need is a lot of cardboard boxes, tape, hot glue, and scissors. You can get cardboard for free or pretty cheap at most big box stores and supermarkets. They often have pre-flattened bales of it, which is really useful for your project, and if they aren't free, you can generally buy a large bundle that weighs over fifty pounds for a couple dollars. This should be plenty of cardboard for a standard sized rental. There are a thousand tutorials online for making various cardboard furniture projects. You can buy a big bundle of hot glue at your local hobby store along with a hot glue gun for fewer than ten dollars. For the tape, general paper-like scotch tape. There is actual cardboard tape that is sold by packing companies, and it looks like it is made out of a brown paper bag. However, this is a little more expensive, and completely unnecessary because it will be covered anyway. I'm fairly certain you know where to buy scissors if you don't already have some. Make sure to get strong ones, as cardboard is hard to cut through and rough on standard scissors.

When you are covering this furniture, make sure not to use something water based, especially if painting. You do not want the cardboard to warp. You can cover it in fabric, stapling it down, or you can wallpaper it. There are a lot of options out there for making it look like real furniture.

The upside to cardboard furniture is that it is easy to move, and if made right, it is actually pretty durable, however, if you are just making it stage, and you don't make it strong, it is easily damaged when someone goes to sit down, so make sure to tell people viewing the house that the furniture is simply propped furniture, and not to lean on it unless you took the extra time to make it strong and durable.

If you are staging a house and leaving the furniture, then you need something that is a little more real than cardboard furniture. However, it does not have to be high end. Free furniture advertised in ads online works quite well as long as it is in good condition, and has been thoroughly checked for bedbugs. Often times, you can go in the alley by the dumpsters behind furniture stores, and you will find brand new beds and chairs just thrown out because they got a little stain on them or a tiny tear in the upholstery. These are the best because they are in almost brand new condition aside from a few little cosmetic issues that are easily fixed, and maybe being a little dirty from being in the alley. Garage sales and moving sales are also a great way to get furniture and appliances for a low price. You can generally get good quality things from these sales, and they won't break the bank. You don't have to have matching furniture, but if you can find matching sets for a good price, then, by all means, snatch it up, because the more cohesive it looks, the more desirable it is. However, chances are, if the tenants need a furnished property, the will not mind if the couch is a different color than the armchair, as long as they don't clash.

If you can't find free furniture, or any garage sales or moving sales, then look online and at liquidation outlets. Online you can buy second-hand furniture for cheap, and there are groups on Facebook that are literally called online garage sales. They are especially useful in the winter months when garage sale season is pretty much over. You can still find furniture and appliances for a good price. However, if you can't find any there, then you should look at liquidation outlets.

Liquidation outlets are going to be a little pricier because you are getting brand new items for a lower price, but not second-hand low. However, it is still less expensive than big box stores. You can buy some good furniture that maybe isn't name brand for a good price and set up your property elsewhere.

If you can't find any of these, maybe it is best to not furnish your home and just stick with cardboard staging. You don't want to break the bank for furniture that you will probably have to replace when your tenants move out.

When furnishing the house, however, always give the tenants the option to bring their own furniture, and provide them a place to store what is already in there if they need to. A lot of people prefer to have their own furniture unless they do not have any furniture of their own. These people are few and far between unless you live in a college town, and then it is a bunch of young adults' house sharing, and most of them don't have their own furniture, so they look for pre-furnished housing. However, in a general area, the only people that need a furnished house is someone who was homeless and recently got a job and needs a place to live, people who lost their home to a disaster, and people escaping abusive relationships. There are a few exceptions, but those are the general reasons.

Always keep the place clean and shined up. If you have a showing that day, go in a half hour early to dust and sweep up and run a bit of furniture polish over the woods in the house. This just gives the house a brighter feel and will make it more appealing to people who are walking through, because everyone wants to move into a nice clean house, and when you show it to them when it is shiny, they will instantly be more attracted to it. Keeping everything gleaming will get your property rented out faster than you would think.

Those are the tips to getting your house ready to show. This is the most rigorous process; it gets a little easier. However, there are still a few tips about being a good landlord and picking the right tenants.

Chapter 4: Picking the Right Tenants

There are a few tips for picking the right tenants and making sure that you will not get played in the end. There is a plethora of good tenants out there, but there are always a few apples in the bunch. Checking the applicants is a great way to make sure that you are not at risk of getting the short end of the stick.

There are a few tips to checking the applicants and where to raise some red flags, and where to proceed as normal. Remember, you have the right to refuse a rental to anyone, just make sure that it is for legitimate reasons, and not discrimination against any race, religion, age, height, weight, or disability. Some states even require you to allow anyone of any marital status live on your property; some do not.

You also have the right to deny any pets, unless they are registered as a service animal. Then you cannot deny the animal, as it is not considered a pet. You are allowed to require proof of the animal being registered. However, you are not allowed to ask for what disability does the animal assist the person. However, the only animals that can be registered right now are dogs and cats. Horses can be registered as therapy animals. However, you are not required to allow a horse to live in your property, as they are only eligible to be registered if the person lives in the proper area. You don't have to worry about someone having a monkey or pygmy pig and saying that you have to allow the animal because it is a service animal. Any documentation that they have is forged, and these people can be reported for fraud.

When you are looking for tenants, make sure to charge a small application fee. This fee will weed out the people who just want to move in for the bare minimum, and who may not have a large enough income to afford your property. It will also be to cover the cost of background and credit checks. You should always run these to decide if your tenant is the right fit for your property. You should also do reference checks on your tenant as well because you need to ensure that they have a good renting history, and are not searching for a new rental due to eviction.

It is important that you meet the people who want to move into your property as well. Always do a walk through with them, and get a look at them, and see if they put in the effort to look nice to meet you. You want someone that is going to take care of your property, and if they are unkempt, they probably will not be able to do so. Dressing nice doesn't mean a three-piece suit; it just means something a little better than holy, stained clothes. If they look clean, and their clothes look well taken care of, that gives you the impression that they are good at taking care of things. However, if their appearance is the only red flag that they have, then you should not hold that against them. They might have just got off work, and didn't have time to change because they did not want to waste your time. You cannot be snobby about their appearance, however, if they didn't want to pay the application fee, and their background, credit, and reference checks come back with negative results, and they look unkempt, then, by all means, say no.

After you run all of the credit checks and find the right tenant, it is time for you to write a contract and start being a landlord. There are some tips for that as well, as you want to be sure that you keep the tenant in the property for as long as possible.

Chapter 5: Becoming a Landlord

Once you have a tenant ready to move into the property, you have to draw up a contract. While you are in the process of looking for a tenant, before you even make a decision, you should do some research on laws in your area involving what you are allowed to put in a contract for leasing, and what you are not. Here are a few federal ones that are mandated across the United States. If you are in a different country, you may have different laws.

You cannot put in a contract anything that requires your tenant to be okay with you entering the property any time that you want. You have to allow them their privacy and give reasonable notice when you want to enter the property. You are not allowed to do "inspections" on the property to check up on how the tenants are treating it. This violates their property. You are able to enter the property to make repairs and make sure that the house does not need anything. When the tenant moves in, that becomes their personal living space, and they are technically buying the house for the months that they are in it.

You cannot place signs on the property without prior written approval from the family. This includes for sale signs and political signs. However, you can put them on the other side of the sidewalk, which is technically city property. Once you cross the sidewalk, that is the tenant's space, and you have to respect that.

You can't force a tenant to pay rent on an unlivable establishment. If something important breaks, and you do not fix it, the establishment is deemed damaged. If that something is a water line or a floor, or a roof, the establishment is deemed unlivable. If this happens, and you do nothing to fix it, the tenant can choose to terminate the contract and move out with no obligation to pay you the rent that they owe on the rest of the contract, as you voided it by not ensuring that the property was livable.

These are some federal laws that are in effect. However, it is in your best interest to do some research on local laws, because laws differ from state to state. The more research you do, the better it will be if you do get stuck with a tenant that refuses to pay, and you have to take the person to court. If there is an infraction in your contract that could skew the odds more into the tenant's favor. You want to protect both your rights, and the tenant's rights, but mainly your rights. So be vigilant in your quest to making a contract up.

If you do not feel confident in your contract writing abilities, you can use a site like LegalZoom, which will help you write up a contract. For a small fee, it will walk you through the process, and help you find the laws for your area in the leasing sector. Or you can have an actual lawyer draw one up, though this can get pricey, it is the most likely to be ironclad.

Also, always get your contracts notarized. This means that you sign in front of a notary, and you have a truly legal piece of paper. It generally costs less than five dollars, and more courts recognize it as a valid contract than one that is not notarized.

Being a Good Landlord

You want to be a good landlord. This means that you have to be an all in person. You have to be hands on, and keep an open line of communication with the tenants. However, you must also respect their privacy. Check in with them on occasion to make sure that everything is going good, but don't be overbearing.

Also, if something breaks, be prompt to fix it or have it fixed. Don't leave your tenants without a dryer if you were the one who supplied the dryer in the first place. Don't make a family go without heat in the middle of winter, just because you don't want to get out in the cold or pay to hire a serviceman to do it for you. You have to do the unpleasant work, along with collecting the rent.

Be understanding, yet firm. If your tenant is running a little late on the rent because their car needs to be fixed, then be understanding. However, if they are late every month, put your foot down, and demands they become more current with their rent. Hard times happen, but you can't let that drain you of your profit. A one-time deal is okay, but not if it happens every month.

Have an emergency fund. If you do not have an emergency fund, how are you going to fix things when they break? If you do not have any money at the time, you are going to get bit in the rear end. You can have your tenants fix it and take it off their rent, but that could be a lot of rent lost if it is a big thing. Otherwise, you may find yourself in a pickle if you don't get it fixed and your tenant has to move because of it. It is always best to take a portion of the money you get from the rent each month and put into an emergency fund to ensure that you will have money to make necessary repairs.

Chapter 6: Do's and Don'ts

This is a business where you want to be on top. You want to make a good impression in order to attract people to you. Not only do you want to attract buyers when you go to sell a house, but you also want to attract sellers when you go to buy a house. There are some sure-fire ways to attract people to you when you want to do anything with your flipping process.

How to Attract Sellers

The first rule is to remember that you are not entitled to getting anything off the asking price. In today's age, so many people go in feeling like they deserve for someone to take their lower offer just because they put the offer in, and this instantly turns a seller off. Another tactic that people have geared towards is going in with everything that is wrong with a property and acting like they are doing the seller a favor for even being interested in it. This is not the way to go. You will not get any leverage this way, and you should remember that it is in your best interest to keep the seller happy.

However, if you play your cards right, you will be able to get the seller to be more open to your offers, rather than sticking with their original asking price, and not wanting to budge. This is something that you just have to use a little finesse to obtain.

When you go in to make a deal, do your best to get a face-to-face meeting with the seller. By asking for a sit-down discussion, the seller can be sure that you are truly interested in the property rather than wasting their time. This will already cause them to be more inclined to want to do business with you. When you go into the meeting, make sure to start with a firm handshake and solid eye contact. This will help you establish a connection with the seller, and you will also be able to gauge how trustworthy they are as well.

Start out by asking them what they have put into the house, and if they have any emotional investment in the property. Seeming interested in why they are selling it will help the seller feel like you are not just there to buy the property; you are there to buy their property. It makes a big difference, even though there is only one word changed in between the sentences.

Tell them all the things you like about the house. Emphasize on them so that the seller knows that you truly are interested. Then go into what needs to be worked on with the property. You could say, "I really love these parts (insert positives here), but I do have a few concerns. (Insert negatives here)" This way you are not completely dogging the property, and the seller will be more open towards negotiating on the bad parts.

Seal the deal with a solid handshake once you reach a comfortable price for both you and the seller. This will help close the deal and ensure that they will not take a higher offer before you close.

Attracting Buyers

When you go to sell your property, you want to sell it fast. This means that you want to attract buyers. There are several ways that you can do this, but this section will focus on the three main ways that you can do so.

Hang Signs

Of course, you want a for sale sign on the front lawn. Make sure that the sign is big enough to attract the attention of people who are driving by. If you are not going through a real estate agent, then you can hang your own sign. Make it decorative and inviting, but keep in mind people are only going to see it for a few seconds tops, so make the writing big and keep it short. Your sign may be what draws people to your property.

Host an Open House

This was briefed upon in a previous chapter, but it should be stressed that an open house shows that you have nothing to hide about the property and that you want people to come in and enjoy it. To really attract people, offer refreshments, and be there the entire time to answer any questions anyone may have. An open house will really get people attracted to your openness and will help you when it comes to selling your property.

Host Meetings with Potential Buyers

When someone is interested in your property, offer to meet him or her face to face and take him or her on an in-depth tour of the property. This will show the potential buyer that they matter, and show them that you are not all about the money. Establishing a connection will make people want to buy your house, probably pretty close to asking price.

As with any subject, there are always dos and don'ts. There are things that you absolutely should do, and things that you absolutely should not do. This chapter will talk about those things through every stage of the process. If you feel like the information in this book is getting a little overwhelming, don't worry. In the next chapter, it will all be broken down into a step-by-step guide to success. But for now, here is a little more information to pad your success rate. The more you know, the better, especially in this business.

Buying a Property

Do: Make sure you do your research. Check out everything that you need to know about the neighborhood, the school district, and the crime rates. Also, check into back taxes. Doing your research will help save you a lot of money in the long run.

Don't: Forge ahead with the negotiation process not knowing what is in store for you. You have to have some idea of what you are getting into in order to make sure that you are getting a good deal and not walking into a money pit. Money pits are the worst, and if your first property is one, you will lose all encouragement to continue.

Do: Get the property inspected before you make any sort of solid deal on the house. The house may look great on the surface, but even the most beautiful house can have a lot of dark secrets hidden among its nooks and crannies. An inspector can tell you if it is worth it to continue on with the negotiation process.

Don't: Jump in with both feet. You always want to make sure that you are making a sound investment. You cannot do that if you get too emotionally invested in a property to the point where you refuse to note that there are flaws that could cost you a lot of money. Make sure that you are making a sound investment, and do not forgo the inspection.

Do: Look for a property that is good for your bottom line. You want to look for a property that takes the least amount of money to gain the most. Or even one that takes a lot of work but is so inexpensive that it is worth it. You want to find a property that helps you grow financially.

Don't: Look for a property that suits you and your family. You are not looking for a second home for you and your family, you are looking for something that brings in extra income for you and your family. Thinking in the way of what suits you can cause you to miss out on a lot of great opportunities.

Working on a House

Do: Find some great materials that are easy on your budget. There are a lot of alternative materials out there that can make the place look great, and be even better for your profit line. You want to go for these materials because again, you are not going to be the one living in it. You want the house to have some appeal, but you do not want it to be complete to your taste, and you do not want to break the bank on renovations.

Don't: Put a lot of expensive, high-end products on your property. Unless you are selling a house in Beverly Hills, you are not going to get enough money to cover the costs of these products from your property. This can severely hurt your bottom line, and the bottom line is what you want to protect. It is better to go with materials that look nice but are not super expensive for the property you are flipping.

Do: Find creative ways to save money where you can on quality products. There are a lot of places that you can go to find great deals on stuff. These places are places such as liquidation outlets, and garage sales. You can also find alternative materials, and repurpose some materials.

Don't: Cut corners to cut costs. This will be noted in an inspection and can hurt your bottom line. People will not want to pay your asking price if you do not do quality work when renovating a house. You have to do quality work and put in the quality product, even if it means paying full price for something.

Do: Add quaint and interesting touches to the house. A pop of color with paint is really an eye attractor, and paint can be easily changed. A feature wall can draw the eye to an area of the house that should be most noted, and can also be changed fairly easily if someone chooses to do so.

Don't: Fashion the whole place in your style. What works for you might not work for other people. It is best to keep most things neutral and add just a splash of style to draw people's attention to things. While you want the property to stand out, not everyone has the same taste as you.

Do: Stage the home with a good amount of style. Add pops of color with pillows and fabrics as well as curtains. People should be able to see themselves in a space, and they should be able to have a good idea of the best possible furniture arrangements.

Don't: Show an empty, barren house. No one can truly imagine themselves in a space that looks like it was made for prison inmates. It is a common misconception that showing an empty house makes the rooms look bigger when in reality, it just makes the house look barren and boring.

Do: Find creative ways to stage your property for a little amount of money. Use your creativity and create furniture, or repurpose old furniture that you can find for cheap. Find good deals at thrift stores and garage sales. Scour the Internet for affordable furniture.

Don't: Buy expensive brand new furniture to stage a house. Because once you sell the house, you are going to have to store that furniture until the next time you sell a house, and that costs money. Anything that costs you money-involving properties is a hit to your profit margin. So go for cheap furniture, it is not going to be there long, and it won't hurt to let it go with the house.

Selling a House

Do: Put it up for sale as soon as you have finished remodeling or staging. Time is money, and money is important in this game. The sooner you have it posted for sale, the better chance you have of selling it quickly, and that is a good thing.

Don't: Put it up for sale before the work is finished. This can cause you to miss out on a lot of opportunities because people will want to see the property right away, and if it is not ready to be shown, they would rather move on than wait for it to be finished.

Do: Host an open house, be present, and bring refreshments. Get to know people, and answer any questions they may have about the house. Give them a number to contact you with any questions.

Don't: Leave someone in charge of your open house who does not know anything about the house. It is best to be there personally so that you can make sure that all questions are answered correctly, and that people are getting a connection with you.

Do: Meet potential buyers face to face. Allow room for negotiation as well. Everyone wants to feel like a winner, and if you both can walk away with a little bit of a win, then you will both feel good.

Don't: Do everything over the phone, and don't be a stickler or a pushover. You have to be lenient on price, but not too lenient because that is your income you are dealing with. You also can't be so firm on the price that negotiating is not possible. You will not sell fast that way.

Chapter 7: Extra Tips for Maximizing Profit

Once you have found a suitable property, and have had it inspected, you can make an offer on the property. It is always pertinent to keep in mind that the seller has to make money too, and if you try to offer too low, you could close them off to any further offers from you.

Yet you still need to make a profit as well. The best way to go is to find a good middle ground, that is towards the lower end of your budget, so you have some negotiation room, but not too low so that you can still continue the negotiation process on the property. A lot of times a seller will not accept the first offer that you throw at them, so you have to find a good middle ground that allows you are negotiating room without going over budget.

When making a negotiation, especially your first, you should have someone there that knows your top dollar and can help you stay within the means of that budget. They will tell you when you should walk away because sometimes it is hard to see for yourself when you need to just cut your losses and walk from the deal and continue your search. Often times, when a person gets into the negotiation, they become committed to getting the property no matter what, and that can cause budget problems that can really hurt your profit.

You should always have the property inspected before you go into the negotiation process. That way you can take the results of the inspection into the negotiation, and use that as leverage to try to get the number down more into your zone. If there is anything wrong with the house that could be a potential problem, then you can use that to try to either get the seller to cover all of the closing costs or cut down the price considerably – either one saves you money. If the seller is already covering closing costs, then you will find that it will be easier to get the ball in your court, because the longer it takes to sell, the more the closing costs are. You want to make sure that you are paying attention to the other party's returns. When they get to where they are not budging much on the price, maybe by a hundred dollars, you have pretty much reached the negotiation limit. It is at that point you can either make one final offer close to their counter or take their counter if it is reasonable.

Negotiations are often tricky, but there are a few things that you should keep in mind when you head into one. These are not necessarily rules, more like guidelines that are important to follow. You want to follow these guidelines as close as you possibly can for most negotiations because this will help you set a solid negotiation foundation.

- **#1 Firm Handshake**

Of course, this only applies when you are meeting the seller in person. However, a firm handshake sets the tone for the entire negotiation and can help the seller be more friendly and open towards your offers. They say first impressions are important, and they truly are, so it is best to start with your best foot, or in this case hand, forward.

- **#2 Never Lowball**

Low-ball offers are the bane of a seller's existence. A good rule of thumb is to never offer below two-thirds of the asking price. Anything under two-thirds is an insulting offer unless you have proof that the house is only worth that much.

- **#3 Don't Seem Too Eager**

Take some time to think over each counter offer that the seller sends back to you. Figure out a good way to counter back, or ponder taking the offer. Never seem like you are willing to do anything to buy the house because that leaves you open to being taken for granted. You want to appear as if you are just buying a property and you couldn't care less if you had to walk from the deal. This will make the seller more interested in appeasing you because they will see that you will not take anything less than a reasonable offer.

Above all, just use common sense when it comes to the negotiation portion of making a deal. There are so many things that you can do when you are negotiating with a seller that will cause them to want help you out, and most of them have to deal with being a good poker player. If you have a good bluff, then you can win a negotiation.

Maximizing Profit

Money, the thing that makes the world go round. It is quite the fickle thing. Misuse it once, and you could have problems that stem from that misuse for a long time. However, play your cards right, and you will find that money is not a problem for you. It all depends on how you play the game of life.

This business is all about the money, the bottom line- the profit. You can't keep this business going if you don't have the profit. You have to have money to buy and flip each house that you are looking into, so each property has to bring in a good amount of profit. There are several ways that you can do this, and each way has its own pros and cons.

- **#1 Stay away from bank loans**

Bank loans seem to be the hardest thing to gain a profit from. While they may help you get a better property because you have access to more money, often times, the interest rates kill any profit you can manage to get, plus having to pay the loan back even if you haven't sold the house yet can cause a lot of problems. The best thing to do is to save up your own money until you get a sizable amount and then you can move on to buying a property to flip. Or you can ask a friend to go in with you and split the profits down the middle. If you find a good enough deal, you will both end up with a good amount of profit, and you can take the profit you made and find another property.

- **#2 Do the work yourself**

A lot of the stuff that needs to be done to a property, you can probably do yourself, unless the property needs an entire overhaul. Cosmetic things such as changing faucets and painting walls, laying floors and hanging cabinets do not take a degree in carpentry to do. All you need is a little elbow grease and maybe a few YouTube videos.

Doing a lot of the work yourself can help you tremendously when it comes to saving money. You do not have to pay labor costs along with the cost of the product because you are doing all of the labor. While it is not a good idea to do electrical, plumbing, or roofing if you do not have previous knowledge, everything else such as framing walls, doing drywall, and all of the updating is fair game. You can save thousands by cutting out the labor costs. These labor costs can help you out towards pocketing profit, because of the less money you put into the house, the better the profit when you sell it.

- **#3 Remember the neighborhood**

A lot of people only focus on the house when they go to do the renovations. They try to make the house look as nice as they possibly can to attract more people, and while making the house look nice is a good thing, there is such a thing as too nice. If you have a house that sticks out in the neighborhood as too fancy, you will bring the value down tremendously, rather than raising it up. This is because the curb appeal actually goes down when your house looks too nice because it sticks out like a sore thumb. By all means, add a fresh coat of paint and fix the broken porch, but don't make the house look like it belongs in a homes and gardens magazine if the rest of the neighborhood doesn't match.

- **#4 Staging is important**

Something that is seen as unimportant can actually help sell your home for a higher price. It does not have to be expensive, a lot of times you can make cardboard furniture to help stage the room, and just add decorative pillows and curtains to go with it.

People want to see themselves in a house, and if they can't see themselves in a house very well, it makes them less apt to give a higher offer. However, if they can see just how well the space works, then they can begin to see their stuff in each room, which will make the house more desirable. You want to make sure that people desire the house and want to offer you what you deserve for the property.

Those are some of the ways that you can maximize your profit when you go to sell your first property. However, there is a massive way that you can save money and make a better profit that has nothing to do with the property at all. It is known as a budget.

Budgeting

Admit it, you kind of cringed at the word. Budgets are seen as a constriction of free will when it comes to money. However, they are necessary for this business to keep you from going overboard with your money. They are necessary for life really. You have to have a budget to ensure that you are making the right moves when it comes to buying and flipping a house. The better you are on a budget, the better your profit margin will be.

There are three things that you should remember when it comes to budgeting. These three things will help you become proficient at creating and maintaining a budget to ensure the maximum amount of profits available. These are mini rules that you can follow to help you out as you learn the ropes of real estate budgeting

- **#1 Split the Budget**

It is not enough to have a budget of money that you cannot go over. If you do that, you run the risk of spending too much in one area, and not having enough for something else, which will often leave you having to go over the amount you intended to for the whole deal.

Instead, you should split your budget up into groups, and allocate a certain amount of the funds to each group. One group can be buying a property, another group could be for renovations, and another smaller group could be for staging the house. Or you could have the third section as emergency funds.

You can split it up into as many groups as you would like however you would like. You should just make sure that you split it up.

- **#2 Know Your Accountability**

If you are not that responsible with money, you should have someone help hold you accountable through the entire process to ensure that you do not go over your budget. It may make you feel silly having someone looking over your shoulder ensuring that you do not spend too much, but it will help hold you accountable until you learn to do that yourself.

You should not be ashamed that you have a hard time managing money. A lot of people have the same problem. The only difference is that you have to learn to manage money pretty quickly so that you can keep yourself from making a flub when it comes to your profit margin. You have to know your level of accountability though. Otherwise, you will not be able to know if you are spending too much. Listen to the input of others around you, and pay attention to how you are in a store. If you buy unnecessary items that you really don't need, then chances are you do not have enough control of your money to go at this alone.

- **#3 Keep Track of Everything**

Every purchase you make should be logged and accounted for. Even if you just bought a box of nails or a pack of batteries for your flashlights. If you are using it for the house, mark it down. This will help you see where all the money is going so that you can make some changes if need be. If you find that you are spending too much on screws and nails, look at the sizes of boxes you are buying, and maybe just go with the bigger boxes to save money in the long run.

By keeping track of every single purchase you make from the time you buy the house (that purchase should be logged too) to the time you sell it, you will be able to get an accurate representation of how much you made in profit, and how much you could have made if you had done things a little differently. You will be able to learn from your mistakes and do better the next time around.

Making a budget is a great way to maximize your

profit because you can be sure not to spend too much on any aspect of the flipping process.

Conclusion

Thank you again for your purchase. Hopefully, you learned everything that you needed to know from reading this book. Do not be afraid to jump into this way of life. It is a great way to free your wallet and your life. You can be a success if you follow the tips in this book. Find a house that works for you, and work up from there. You won't be sorry that you did.

If you liked this book, please leave a good review on Amazon.

www.ingramcontent.com/pod-product-compliance
Lightning Source LLC
Chambersburg PA
CBHW050210230526
45470CB00001B/323